# AMSTERDAM

A Picture Book to Remember Her by

**CRESCENT BOOKS**
**NEW YORK**

CLB 1604
© 1986 Illustrations and text: Colour Library Books Ltd.,
    Guildford, Surrey, England.
Text filmsetting by Acesetters Ltd., Richmond, Surrey, England.
All rights reserved.
Printed and bound in Barcelona, Spain by Cronion, S.A.
1986 edition published by Crescent Books, distributed by Crown Publishers, Inc.
ISBN 0 517 61399 9
h g f e d c b a

Canals, holding the reflections of tall gabled houses, arched bridges and orderly-planted, carefully-tended trees, furnish many of the essential images conjured by Amsterdam in the stranger and carried home by the visitor. The central part of the city, from which these images are drawn, is, largely, a meticulously preserved version of the outlines of Amsterdam in the 17th century.

The shape these visually pleasing outlines take is in fact very functional, dictated by the demands of the trade which was the building force of Amsterdam. The city originated as a small fishing settlement along the banks of the Amstel River, and, by the beginning of the 16th century, had developed into a walled city of about 12,000 inhabitants. This early Amsterdam lay in an ideal position to build up a thriving trade with the Baltic countries in grain, furs and timber, and with France and Portugal in spices, wine and salt.

More far-flung merchant ventures were consolidated in 1602, when the Dutch East India Company – the V.O.C. – was formed, 60 per cent of its capital being provided by companies in Amsterdam. In the enthusiasm and grand confidence which accompanied its creation, the V.O.C. was granted a trading monopoly for all the world east of the Cape of Good Hope, and established bases, for example, in the East Indies, India, the Cape of Good Hope and Japan, making huge profits from trade in 'fine Indian wares of nutmeg, cloves, mace, cinnamon and pepper... linens, silks, fluids, gums, dyes, porcelain and all other merchandise.'

This world-wide network of successful trade brought tremendous pressures of population and commercial activity to the old medieval city, and, by 1562, it was overcrowded and beset by disreputable slums outside the walls. To overcome these problems, Amsterdam's enterprising Municipal Council resolved to remodel their city to fit its supreme function as a centre of sea trade. At the end of the 16th century, 1,336 acres were assigned to be the site of the new city development, and a plan was drawn up designed to provide housing for merchants and immigrants, and to display Amsterdam's wealth and commercial power.

Projected new canals were added to the old Singelgracht, extending Amsterdam's waterfront to cater for the volume of trade and to ease the movement of heavy, bulky goods through the city. The 17th-century canal pattern is still intact in the three wide semicircles of the Herengracht, the Keizersgracht and the Prinsengracht, their concentric curves interlinked by numerous minor, radial canals. Built in straight sections, with angular turns to aid their navigation by barge, more than 600 of the now-familiar brick-lined canals were dug in a period of great, concentrated labour, reaching completion in 1663.

The necessity for land transport and the movement of pedestrians was not forgotten in this grand, water-orientated design, and more than 200 bridges were built in quick succession to the canals. Many of these original, hump-back structures still adorn the waterways, and their construction set the pattern for future centuries of bridge building.

The distinctively tall, narrow canalside houses known to today's visitor were also shaped by the all-pervading demands of trade. The master-plan of the Municipal Council assigned the plots bordering main canals to the city's wealthy merchants, and, to ensure that each acquired a measure of canal frontage, decreed that no house be more than 3 windows' width – roughly 26 feet. Later eased to allow for 5 windows' width, these restrictions forced merchants to extend their mansions upwards to 4 storeys and backwards for up to 180 feet to recover the capacity they had lost to the requirements of trade.

Municipal limitations on the size, shape and even the building materials of their canalside houses encouraged merchants to indulge in modest ostentations, prompting them to imaginative flourishes of individuality in the shaping of the high gables – whether stepped, bell-shaped, or adorned with ornate cornices –; in brickwork decorated with sculptures; in the colourful, bas-relief gable plaques depicting the owner's occupation or character, even in the disguising of the functional hoisting beam in fanciful designs.

So much of this purpose-built trade city of the 17th century has survived intact, initially because of the decline in Amsterdam's fortunes during the industrial revolution, when the city could not afford any redevelopment. When her trade revived this century, Amsterdam's people had come to value their antique city, and today the work of ardent conservationists and city legislation has ensured that the exteriors of many 17th-century buildings, and their surroundings of canals, bridges and tree-lined avenues, have been preserved intact. Today, canal-side houses may be converted inside for use as offices, restaurants, art galleries or museums, and still constitute very much the living centre of Amsterdam.

Facing page: the Keukenhof Gardens in Lisse, southwest of Amsterdam.

Dep. Leg. B-18.998-86

Left: shoppers in the Muntplein. Far left: a backstreet off the Waterlooplein. Below: houses on Kromme Waal Street. Facing page: (top right) the bronze statue of an urchin grins cheekily across Spui Square; (top left) a canal in the city centre, flanked by the attractive, narrow, gabled houses so characteristic of Amsterdam; (bottom) a variety of boats and barges throw their colourful reflections on the smooth waters of the Waals Eilandsgracht. Overleaf: a barge plies its way along one of the city's canals.

Below and right: gaily painted barges moored on the Oosterdok. The wooden Magere Brug drawbridge (bottom) is over 300 years old and is still in use today. It spans the Amstel River, around which the city developed and from which it derived its name. Facing page: a tranquil canal scene. Overleaf: one of the many bridges spanning the Reguliersgracht.

Above: the 17th century House of Three Canals. By night the city is aglow with dazzling neon displays (top) and illuminated bridges and streets, such as those (top left) shimmering on the Amstel River. Centre left: the Singel Canal, with (left) one of the popular launches that provide an excellent way of seeing the city. Far left: a floating shanty nestling by a bridge.

Amsterdam's attractive stores make shopping a real pleasure. Top: a shop selling colourful clogs. Top left: a tempting delicatessen. The markets are also delightful, with their glorious flower stalls (facing page) and age-old customs, such as those upheld at the Alkmaar cheese market (left). Above: due to the narrowness of staircases in the city's old houses, delivery and removal of bulky objects must often be made via the windows.

Previous pages: (left) the
Mint Tower, (right) Hotel de
l'Europe on the Singel Canal.
Above: tourists and visitors
alike enjoy the friendly
atmosphere of an Amsterdam
café. Right: feeding pigeons
in Dam Square, which stands on
the site of the dam that was
built across the Amstel in the
13th century. Below: trams are
a convenient and picturesque
mode of transport. Facing
page: the Tea Garden Herb Shop
behind the Rijksmuseum.

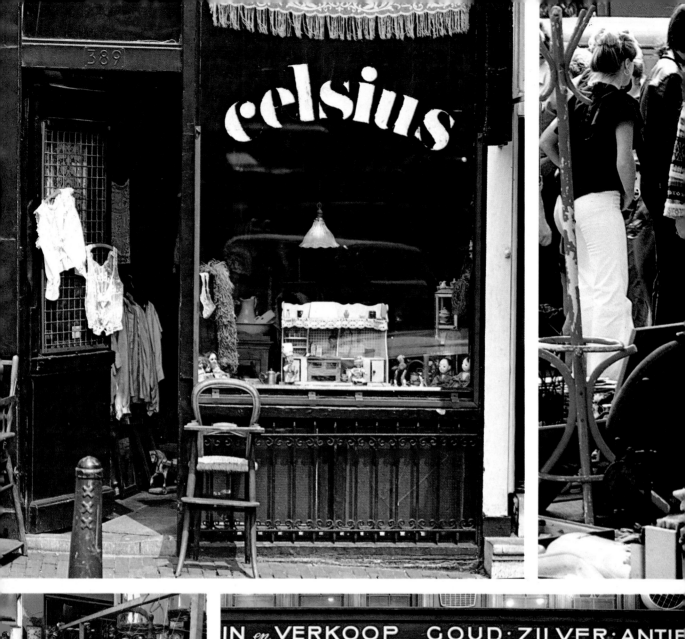

Previous pages: the colourful bustle of city life. Above: a cosy café near Dam Square. Fascinating bric-a-brac can be found at the flea market in the Waterlooplein (top centre) and in the many quaint shops (these pages), whose contents seem as old as their facades.

These pages: cycling is a popular form of transport in Amsterdam due to the city's gentle slopes and narrow, congested streets. Facing page and overleaf: a mural brightens a canalside building.

Many houseboats, with their stylish, comfortable interiors (right and top) and beautifully kept gardens (top centre), are every bit as homely as conventional houses (above and far right). Top right: Rembrandt House, where the artist lived for 21 years.

Above: Damrak Harbour, overlooked by the decorative facade of Central Station, which was designed by P.J.H. Cuypers, who also designed the Rijksmuseum. Top right: tourist-packed sightseeing cruisers on the Rokin Canal. Right: a mother plays with her child inside a cosy houseboat. Far right: a sleek houseboat moored on the lovely Prinsengracht. Overleaf: the view of the city's tree-lined canals and charming, gabled roofs from the tower of the Westerkirk (Western Church).

Far left: a downstream view of the Amstel River, with the Magere Bridge in the distance. Above: the imposing Montelbaans Tower rises from the edge of the Oudeschans Canal. The houses (left) overlooking the Singel Canal are typical of the city's 17th century canal-side buildings, which were designed with tall, many-windowed facades so as to meet the demand for views of the water.

Right: the Van Baerlestraat
Concert Hall. Below: the Mint
Tower at sunset. Bottom: the
Schiller Restaurant of 1892,
one of the few buildings on
the Rembrandtsplein to have
survived the war. Facing page:
the magnificent dome of the
Royal Palace (overleaf), which
was originally the town hall
and was converted into a
palace by Napoleon in 1808.

Above: cruise boats in Damrak Harbour. Left: daffodils flourish in the gardens belonging to the 14th and 17th century houses of the Begijnhof. Top: houses enhanced by a type of gable called Halsgevel. Overleaf: one of the city's many lovely parks.

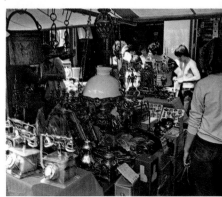

A fine range of Dutch and imported produce is found in the city's delicatessens (top left) and markets (left and centre left). Far left: the Wimpy, a popular British import. Junk shops (top and above) provide an excuse for hours of browsing.

Far left: a souvenir shop in the Langebrugsteeg. Bottom far left and previous pages: an array of cacti in the floating flower stall on the Singel Canal. Among the treasures in the Rijksmuseum (above) is a series of glorious stained glass windows (remaining pictures and overleaf left) depicting famous artists. Overleaf right: a triple-arched bridge spanning a tranquil canal.

Amsterdam assumes a magical and romantic aspect when floodlit at night. Facing page: a bridge spanning the Herengracht at its intersection (previous pages) with the Reguliersgracht. Below: the Magere Bridge. Right: the Mint Tower. Dazzling neon lights (above) add to the excitement of the city's nightlife.

Below: a striking piece of modern sculpture in the Stedelijk Museum. Right: one of several group portraits of the old civic guards of Amsterdam housed in the Civic Guard Gallery of the Amsterdam Historical Museum. Remaining pictures: the famous Van Gogh Museum, which is dedicated to the works of Vincent Van Gogh and his contemporaries.

Previous pages: a sightseeing launch on the Herengracht. Below: delicately-coloured dried flowers arranged attractively in the floating flower market on the Singel Canal. Succulent fresh fruit (centre left) and the vibrant colours of fresh flowers (bottom left) brighten the city's streets and the market near the Mint Tower (left). One of Amsterdam's many charming traditions is the playing of barrel-organ music in the streets. Today, most of these decorative instruments are run by petrol-driven motors but the elaborately fashioned example (far left) is operated by hand.

Below: a game of cards provides a break for two flea market stall holders. Left: the Singel Canal, coloured by the city's lights. Bottom: a power boat provides an exciting way of touring the city's canals. Facing page: the lovely Saint Nicolaas Kirk rises above harbourside homes. Overleaf: an elegant drawbridge.